Alonzo Williams

Rhode Island Day at the World's Columbian Exposition,

Chicago, Illinois,

October the fifth, eighteen hundred and ninety-three

Alonzo Williams

Rhode Island Day at the World's Columbian Exposition, Chicago, Illinois,
October the fifth, eighteen hundred and ninety-three

ISBN/EAN: 9783337380359

Printed in Europe, USA, Canada, Australia, Japan

Cover: Foto ©ninafisch / pixelio.de

More available books at **www.hansebooks.com**

D. Russell Brown

Rhode Island Day

AT

The World's Columbian Exposition

CHICAGO, ILLINOIS

OCTOBER THE FIFTH

EIGHTEEN HUNDRED AND NINETY-THREE

EDITED BY

ALONZO WILLIAMS

RHODE ISLAND'S GIFT

Last of the thirteen, smallest of them all,
What canst thou bring to this World's Festival,
Where all thy sisters come with pride and power,
And bring each one a Princess' generous dower
Of gold and gems, and fruits, and precious woods,
And joyous tribute of their costly goods?
What can we bring? No outward show of gain,
No pomp of state; we bring the sons of men !

Bring gold, fair sisters, yellow gold,
    And gems, and all that's fair and fine,
And heap them all, the new, the old,
    Before our country's stately shrine.
Bring hardihood from north and east,
    Bring beauty from the south and west,
Bring valor to adorn the feast,
    Bring all that has withstood time's test.
We grudge you not the riches rare,
    We grudge you not your acres broad,
We bring you for our noble share
    THE LIBERTY TO WORSHIP GOD.

Caroline Hazard.

CONTENTS

I. General Introduction

The exercises of Rhode Island Day at the World's Columbian Exposition, October 5, 1893, were under the guidance of the Committee on Ceremonies, appointed by the Board of World's Fair Managers of Rhode Island. This committee consisted of:

Hon. John P. Sanborn, *Chairman,*

Arthur H. Watson,   Lorillard Spencer,

Lyman B. Goff,   Gardiner C. Sims.

The arrangements for the day had been made with care and foresight, and every contingency so clearly anticipated that success but waited to crown the efforts of the committee.

The day broke clear and beautiful. All the elements seemed to conspire in favor of the occasion, awaited with such impatience by every loyal son and daughter of Rhode Island. Not a cloud obscured the heavens. The sun put on his brightest robes. The very breezes from the lake tempered the biting chill of yesterday and brought only draughts of inspiration. Good nature, enthusiasm, patriotism, ruled the assembled hosts, and every one seemed satisfied with himself, his neighbors and the world. No such day had smiled upon any State occasion thus far since the Great Fair commenced. Nor had any State Day been honored by such a gathering of the tribes as came up to the great festival. One hundred and seventy-nine thousand, nine hundred and sixty-five was the number of paid admissions to Jackson Park, a number unequalled on any previous State Day. Glowing and complimentary editorials in all the leading daily papers of Chicago had heralded the event, and not only the people of that great city, but the thousands from the East and West, from the North and South, were out to greet the smallest gem in the constellation of sister States that make up the Great Republic. All were arrayed in holiday attire, men and women, old and young, all in harmony with the glad occasion, prepared to hail and applaud and honor "Little Rhody," as they delighted to call her.

Early the members of the Governor's personal and general staff, and the ladies and gentlemen of the official party, began to assemble at the Hotel Auditorium, the Governor's headquarters; and at

11:30 A. M. the line of carriages, containing Gov. Brown and party, and the Commissioners for Rhode Island, was drawn up on Michigan avenue in front of the hotel and proceeded immediately over the grand boulevards to the Fair Grounds. At the Fifty-Seventh street entrance to the Park the Newport Artillery was found drawn up in line, awaiting the arrival of the Governor, whom they received with fitting military honors, and then promptly wheeled into platoons, ready to escort the Governor through the Park to the Rhode Island building. It seemed very appropriate and fitting that this ancient and honorable company, now the oldest active military organization in the United States,—a company chartered in 1741 by King George the Second,—a company born of the troublous times inaugurated by the declaration of war between England and Spain in 1739 and continued by the war between England and France in 1744,—a company that has participated in every war and been present at every siege from that of Fort William Henry in 1757 to that of Petersburg in 1865,—a company that furnished its quota of men in the French and Indian War, and more than *One Thousand* during the Civil War,—a company that served as escort to Governor Arthur Fenner and the General Assembly on Inauguration Day in 1793, and has performed the same service

2

annually even to the present day,—it seemed specially fitting that this venerable company should have the honor of acting as escort to Governor Brown upon a State occasion of such historic importance. The company seemed mindful of its ancient virtue, and every officer and man inspired by the memories of a glorious past. The neat dress uniforms and helmets, the bright scarlet trappings, the soldierly bearing and the marching of the men won the admiration of the crowds that lined the way, and called forth encomiums from the regular army officers present.

Under the inspiring music of the Newport Band the line moved past the State Buildings of South Dakota, Nebraska, Minnesota, Louisiana, Missouri, Pennsylvania, New York and Massachusetts to the Rhode Island State Building. All the State flags were flying and the buildings were decorated in honor of "Little Rhody," and it seemed as though the big States could not show affection enough for their little pet sister. Pennsylvania covered herself all over with gay colors and bunting of red and white and blue, and as if to bestow her highest favor, she tolled the old Liberty Bell as Governor Brown passed her house, while at the same time there came floating on the quiet noon air the sounds of the Peace Bell, located in the Administration Plaza.

When the party arrived at the Rhode Island Building, Hon. John P. Sanborn, Chairman of the Committee on Ceremonies, welcomed Governor Brown and made a formal presentation of the structure to the Governor, who in a brief and fitting speech accepted the building in behalf of the State. Here had already gathered many hundred guests from Rhode Island, ladies and gentlemen, and scores of happy children added their joy to the occasion, and the snug little building, nestling under the right wing of the spacious Hancock House, had on her brightest garments, and festoons of red, white and blue lent gaiety and picturesqueness to the severer lines of her classical architecture. From the staff above the building floated, more proudly than its wont, the emblem of the State, and within was unfurled for the first time at the Fair the old flag carried by Gen. Nathanael Greene's command during the Revolutionary War. The crowd that thronged the building and decked the lawn adorned itself with a badge of light blue, distributed by the genial Col. Wyman, to distinguish the true sons and daughters of Rhode Island from the great outside throng which surged past or stopped a moment to gaze and wonder, and to inquire whether perchance anybody had been left to guard the State at home.

While the line was at rest, the Rhode Island Board of World's Fair Managers tendered a complimentary luncheon to Governor Brown and staff and other invited guests. The New York State Commissioners performed a most graceful act of courtesy in tendering for this purpose the use of the spacious banquet hall in the New York building, opposite. Seventy-five covers were laid and the luncheon was an elaborate one, and its enjoyment enhanced by the very gracious speech of welcome from the New York Commissioner, Hon. Louis M. Howland.

RHODE ISLAND

II. THE MARCH TO MUSIC HALL

At 2 o'clock the line was formed which was to escort Governor Brown to Music Hall, where the exercises of the afternoon were to take place.

THE ORDER OF FORMATION :

Platoon of Columbian Guards, 50 men in gray uniform.

In carriages :

E. Benjamin Andrews, D.D., LL.D., President of the Board of World's Fair Managers.

COMMITTEE ON CEREMONIES :

John P. Sanborn, *Chairman*,	Arthur H. Watson,
Lyman B. Goff,	Lorillard Spencer.

RHODE ISLAND COMMISSIONERS :

Hiram Howard,	Daniel B. Pond,
	Richard Thornley.

EXECUTIVE COMMISSIONER :

John C. Wyman.

Newport Band, 28 pieces, Thos. W. Henry, Leader.

Company Buglers.

Lieut.-Col. Alvin A. Barker, Commanding.

H. C. Stevens, Jr., Adjutant.

Commissioned Staff.

"Old Glory," Gen. Burnside's Headquarters' Flag,
Sergeant Thos. H. Lawton, Bearer.
Newport Artillery, 11 officers and 72 men.
Co. A, Major Geo. C. Shaw.
Company Colors.
Co. C, Lieut. John D. Richardson.
Co. B, Capt. Herbert Bliss.
Non-Commissioned Staff.
In Carriages :
State Colors.
His Excellency, D. Russell Brown, Governor.
Lieut.-Gov. Melville Bull.
Hon. J. W. Horton, Ex-Mayor of Newport.

GENERAL AND PERSONAL STAFF :

Gen. Charles R. Dennis,   Gen. John C. Budlong,
Gen. Charles A. Wilson,   Col. Hunter C. White,
Col. H. Martin Brown,   Col. Raymond G. Mowry,
Col. William B. Waterman,   Col. John H. Wetherell,
Col. Walter H. Stearns,   Col. Frank Harris,
Lieut.-Col. W. Howard Walker,   Lieut.-Col. Geo. H. Kenyon,
Lieut.-Col. Walter R. Stiness,   Capt. Thompson, U. S. A.,
Lieut. Frederick Wooley, U. S. A.

Carriage containing
Professor Alonzo Williams, the Orator of the Day.
Henry R. Palmer, the Poet of the Day.
Col. William A. James, President of Society of Sons and
Daughters of Rhode Island.
Richard W. Jennings, Executive Secretary.

Carriages containing among others :
Miss Charlotte F. Daily, Secretary and Treasurer of the
Board of World's Fair Managers.

Mrs. George A. Mumford,   Mrs. Amey M. Starkweather,
Miss Loraine P. Bucklin, of the Government Commissioners,
Mrs. D. Russell Brown,   Miss Hope C. Brown,
Mrs. H. Martin Brown,   Miss Isabel R. Brown,
Mrs. John P. Sanborn,   Miss Jennie Eddy,
Miss Florence Sanborn,   Mrs. Frank Harris,
Mrs. Alvin A. Barker,   Mrs. Francis P. Kendall,
Miss Maud Pond,   Miss Nannie Pond,
Mrs. C. M. Bull,   Miss Jane W. Kendall,
Mrs. Arthur H. Watson,   Mrs. Walter R. Stiness,
Gen. Hiram Kendall,   Mrs. John H. Wetherell,
Mrs. Hiram Kendall,   Miss Addie S. Warfield,
Col. A. C. Landers,   Mrs. A. C. Landers,
Lieut.-Col. Arthur V. Warfield.

There were in all twenty-five or thirty carriages, containing about one hundred distinguished ladies and gentlemen from Rhode Island, and behind these marched nearly a thousand loyal sons and daughters, all forming a most gratifying and imposing pageant. One of the most attractive features of the procession was the headquarters' flag, "Old Glory," used by Gen. Ambrose E. Burnside during the Civil War, now a trophy of the War Department, but loaned for the day by Capt. John F. Rogers, a former Rhode Islander and nephew of Commodore Oliver Hazard Perry, who now has charge of the Quartermaster's section in the War Department exhibit. The flag was escorted to the Rhode Island building in charge of a guard of regulars and turned over to Executive Commissioner John C. Wyman, and by him entrusted to Lieut.-Col. Alvin A. Barker, who detailed Ordnance Sergeant Thomas H. Lawton, a veteran of the Civil War, to be its bearer and special guardian. Thus are even the mute participants of that great struggle cared for and honored. More than one maimed hero of the Ninth Corps lifted his hat as "Old Glory" passed that day, and as memory ran back up the checkered years something moist stole down the bronzed and furrowed cheek. The compiler of this record cannot forbear to mention in this connection, that beside him in the carriage rode in that triumphal procession a brave son of Rhode Island, who served her well when brave sons were of more worth than gold, Col. William A. James, of the Third Rhode Island Cavalry, who spoke so eloquently that day in behalf of the "Sons and Daughters of Rhode Island," of whose society in Chicago he was the president. Col. James that day was at the very summit of a well-developed manhood, the envy of many who looked upon him. Since then he has been suddenly stricken down and his many friends left to mourn, and to marvel at the mysterious ways of destiny.

The procession wound past the State Buildings

of New Jersey, Connecticut, New Hampshire, Maine, and uncoiled its length upon the Lake Front, passing in succession the stately structures of France, Germany, Spain and Canada, leaving the battleship "Illinois" on the left and the Government Building and the Manufacturers Building on the right, until after a march of one and a half miles it entered the Court of Honor and reached Music Hall, which forms the northern end of the Peristyle. The great white palaces of Jackson Park never looked more imposing and beautiful than under the bright rays of that Indian Summer sun, which shone in all its splendor from a cloudless sky, and the Park itself was radiant in blue and scarlet and gold. Immense crowds lined the way from the beginning to the end of the march, and it has been estimated that fifty thousand spectators greeted "Little Rhody" and her Governor as they passed. The scene will not be soon effaced from the memory of those who were so fortunate as to gaze upon it.

3

III.   EXERCISES AT MUSIC HALL

The spacious auditorium of Music Hall was thronged with a distinguished and inspiring audience, numbering not less than three thousand people. The Newport Band was stationed at the rear of the stage, and on the right and left in front were unfurled the Governor's colors and "Old Glory." When all was ready, His Excellency, Governor Brown, was escorted to the platform by the Committee on Ceremonies, while the band played "Hail to the Chief" and the audience rose, mid applause. Following His Excellency came the members of the official party, ladies and gentlemen, one hundred and fifty in number. Upon the stage were among others:

His Excellency, D. Russell Brown, Governor.
Members of the General and Personal Staff, in full dress uniform.
BOARD OF WORLD'S FAIR MANAGERS OF RHODE ISLAND:
E. Benjamin Andrews, D.D., LL.D., President.
Arthur H. Watson, Vice-President.

Hiram Howard,	Richard Thornley,
Walter A. Peck,	Marsden J. Perry,
Daniel B. Pond,	John P. Sanborn.

GOVERNMENT COMMISSIONERS:

| Lyman B. Goff, | Mrs. Amey M. Starkweather, |
| Gardiner C. Sims, | Miss Charlotte F. Dailey. |

ALTERNATES:

| Jeffrey Hazard, | Mrs. George A. Mumford, |
| Lorillard Spencer, | Miss Loraine P. Bucklin. |

EXECUTIVE COMMISSIONER:

John C. Wyman.

Hon. Melville Bull, Lieutenant-Governor.

Professor Alonzo Williams, Orator.

Henry R. Palmer, Poet.

Col. William A. James, President of "Society of Sons and Daughters of Rhode Island."

MILITARY GUESTS:

| Gen. Hiram Kendall, | Lieut.-Col. Arthur V. Warfield, |

Col. William F. Reynolds, of the Executive Staff of Gov. Pattison, Penn.

Capt. Joseph P. Cotton,	Major T. H. Rathbun,
Capt. Thompson, U. S. A.,	Lieut. Frederick Wooley, U. S. A.
Officers Newport Artillery.	Major Frank H. Harcourt,

OTHER GUESTS:

Col. William Goddard,	Rev. David H. Greer,
Hon. Lucius B. Darling,	Hon. Warren O. Arnold,
Hon. Adin B. Capron,	Hon. Henry J. Spooner,
Hon. Henry R. Barker,	Hon. J. W. Horton,
Hon. Henry L. Greene,	Hon. Albert C. Landers,
Hon. Charles H. Burdick,	Hon. Eugene F. Warner,
Hon. Joseph C. Church,	Hon. Nathan D. Pierce,

Col. Frank F. Olney,
Dr. William H. Palmer,
Dr. C. F. Barker,
William Corliss,
Mrs. D. Russell Brown,
Mrs. Arthur H. Watson,
Miss Hope C. Brown,
Miss Isabel R. Brown,
Mrs. H. Martin Brown.
Miss Jennie Eddy,
Mrs. Nathan D. Pierce,
Miss Louise Sweetland,
Miss Maud Pond,
Miss Harriet C. Balch,
Mrs. William Corliss,
Miss Irene Butler,
Mrs. William F. Reynolds,
Mrs. Hiram Kendall,
Mrs. Walter R. Stiness,
Mrs. John H. Wetherell,
Miss Addie S. Warfield,
Mrs. John C. Budlong,
Mrs. Lucius B. Darling,

Col. Elisha H. Rockwell,
Cornelius S. Sweetland,
Charles E. Harvey,
D. M. Thompson,
Mrs. Warren O. Arnold,
Mrs. Adin B. Capron,
Mrs. John P. Sanborn,
Miss Caroline C. Greene,
Miss Florence Sanborn,
Mrs. Albert C. Landers,
Mrs. Joseph P. Cotton,
Mrs. Alvin A. Barker,
Miss Nannie Pond,
Mrs. Frank F. Olney,
Miss Florence Olney,
Mrs. Daniel J. Sully,
Mrs. Irving Champlin,
Mrs. Francis P. Kendall,
Miss Jane W. Kendall,
Mrs. Frank Harris,
Mrs. C. M. Bull,
Mrs. Dr. Von Gottschalk.

The centre of the hall was occupied by the Newport Artillery. On the right were the members of "The Society of the Sons and Daughters of Rhode Island" residing in Chicago, and behind them was a body of the Alumni of Brown University, many of them now distinguished judges, lawyers, professors, divines, physicians and merchants in Chicago

and neighboring cities. The remaining seats were
filled by many citizens and their families who had
come from Rhode Island. The description of the
audience is, however, not yet complete. A unique
feature of the celebration was the high compliment
paid to Rhode Island and to His Excellency, Governor Brown personally, by the National Commissioners, who were that day in session at Jackson
Park. The Commission adjourned the sitting at the
Administration Building and marched in a body to
Music Hall to pay their respects to Governor Brown
and to the State which he with such dignity represented. The incident was remarkable, inasmuch
as this was the first occasion when the National
Commission had taken part in the celebration of
a State Day, and Rhode Island and her Governor
did not fail to appreciate the courtesy and honor.
When in the midst of the exercises their unexpected
arrival was announced, Governor Brown sent his
Chief of Staff and Executive Commissioner, John
C. Wyman, to meet them and escort them to the
platform. They brought with them the Mexican
Band and the Hungarian Orchestra, and both these
bands added much to the enjoyment of the occasion
by rendering at intervals patriotic and national
airs. Among the fifty or sixty National Commis-
missioners present were :

Gen. Thomas W. Palmer, President of the National Commission.

M. H. DeYoung, of California, Vice-President of the National Commission.

Gorton W. Allen, of New York, Vice-President of the National Commission.

John T. Dickenson, of Texas, Secretary of the National Commission.

Mark L. McDonald, of California.

William Lindsay, of Kentucky.

Frederick J. V. Skiff, of Colorado.

George W. Massey, of Delaware.

LaFayette Funk, of Illinois.

Thomas E. Proctor, of Massachusetts.

George H. Barbour, of Michigan.

James H. Breslin, of New York.

William Ritchie, of Ohio.

Virginius D. Groner, of Virginia.

J. W. St. Clair, of West Virginia.

Walter Aiken, of New Hampshire.

Charles H. Jones, of Missouri.

Elijah B. Martindale, of Indiana.

Charles H. Deere, of Illinois.

Lyman B. Goff, of Rhode Island.

Lorillard Spencer, of Rhode Island.

Such a distinguished gathering as completely filled the stage was in itself a most imposing audience quite worthy of the august occasion.

Programme of the Literary Exercises

Music: Newport Band.

COLUMBIAN FANTASIA, AND CORNET SOLO, BY THOS. W. HENRY.

Address of Welcome.

E. BENJAMIN ANDREWS, PRESIDENT OF THE BOARD
OF WORLD'S FAIR MANAGERS.

Ladies and Gentlemen:—As president of the Rhode
Island World's Fair Commission, it is my honorable duty to open the exercises of this auspicious
day. Be assured, one and all, that you are very
welcome. Your Excellency, who distinguish this
occasion by your official presence; other members
of our State government; representatives of our
State in Congress and of our various city gov-
ernments; citizens of Rhode Island still resident
within her borders; former residents now hailing
from afar; guests who are fain to dry the sweat of
your brows in summer by the cool breezes of our
Narragansett Bay; and any others who may have

honored us by attending, in the name of Rhode Island and of her World's Fair Commission, I bid you heartiest welcome to these festivities.

Rhode Island and the Union—that is the thought which fills the minds of all present at this moment. Ladies and Gentlemen : I need not tell any of you that territorially Rhode Island is small. So was Rome during the years of her proudest deeds. So was Athens, always. So were Macedon, and Phœnicia, and Palestine. States are not great or small according to their miles. And, as the little birth-town of the Christ, Bethlehem, in the land of Juda, was not least among the princes of Juda, so Rhode Island, diminutive as she is physically, is far from least among the princely constituents of this re-public.

Rhode Island glories in having been one of the old thirteen—the first, whether by declaration or by overt act, to renounce allegiance to George III. She founded the American navy, and its most splendid achievement to date stands eternally associated with a Rhode Island name. All the world knows how, in the person of Oliver Hazard Perry at the immortal battle of Lake Erie, we of Rhode Island "met the enemy and they were ours." In sending Washington his best subordinate commander in the Revolutionary War, 'the matchless Nathanael

Greene, Rhode Island had great part also in found-
ing our army. As an early constitution-framer,
Stephen Hopkins is worthy to be classed with Benjamin Franklin. If our State was slow to enter the
Union—long deliberation before action being a
marked characteristic of our people—our record
of services to the Union since we joined it is writ
large on every page of the nation's history.

Not a battlefield between the oceans where brave
men have died for the flag, whose sod is not the
greener for Rhode Island blood.

Rhode Island inventions and manufactories are
known and praised far as civilization has set foot.

In the building and sailing of those merchant
fleets which gave the United States business marine
its brilliant lustre, now dimmed, but to blaze again;
and as well in the creation of our inland commerce,
affording that providential education which taught
our constitution to read nationally,—that divine
cement which made disunion impossible in the day
of national trial,—the good wrought for this nation
by Rhode Island was indefinitely out of proportion
to the number of her souls or her acres.

We have sent forth innumerable sturdy and en-
terprising citizens to help people the old states and
the new.

We have furnished education for multitudes from

4

other states, who have sought it in our institutions of learning.

Many teachers of the nation and of the world in best things are of our own production, among whom I name as specimens Roger Williams, William Ellery Channing, Francis Wayland, Horace Mann, Henry Wheaton, James B. Angell and Rowland Gibson Hazard, grandfather of the gifted poetess whose lines you will soon hear with delight.

Notwithstanding, therefore, the lofty and true words in praise of other states with which, on their respective festal days, this air has rung, we are not ashamed to-day, but very proud instead, to throw to the breezes of Lake Michigan Rhode Island's flag, and to let all the states and nations here assembled know that it ripples in honor of the commonwealth where we have our home and do our work.

However, Ladies and Gentlemen, the nation is greater than any state, and every true Rhode Islander finds it his chief inspiration to-day that what our State has accomplished has not ended with herself but has brought strength and riches to the common life of this magnificent America of ours, whom some now here will live to behold marching, if indeed she is not there already, at the very van of the world's civilization.

And then, peaceable and puissant among the

nations, persuading peace if we can, compelling it
if we must, it will be ours to inaugurate the era of
which the great laureate sings :

> " Where the war drums throb no longer,
>   And the battle flags are furled,
>   In the parliament of man,
>   The federation of the world."

Music : Newport Band.

ZAMPA,   -   -   - -   -   HEROLD.

Address.

His Excellency, D. Russell Brown, Governor.

Mr. President of the Rhode Island Board of Managers of the World's Columbian Exposition, Ladies and Gentlemen :—

This is Rhode Island's Day, the day set apart by the managers of the world's unrivalled exhibition on which Rhode Island citizens may call special attention to her history and her products.

We, the representatives of the smallest and oldest sovereign State of our Union, are assembled here to take up the strains of that glorious anthem of praise and patriotism whose glowing harmonies from the throats of sister commonwealths have reverberated amid the walls of these palaces since their gates were first opened. We are here from the Eastern shores bearing glad greeting and congratulations to our brother freemen of this wonderful city, upon the magnificent success which has attended the fulfilment of a conception as audacious as it is inspiring.

We know it is the greeting of a State whose area
is insignificant compared with the almost boundless
expanse of other States, but we ask you to-day to
overlook that familiar fact, and to take the broader
view of Rhode Island which her age and her history unfolds, for that is the mental picture which
Rhode Islanders always bear of their beloved commonwealth, an image stimulating a strong feeling
of loyalty and exalted local pride, which perhaps
seems somewhat peculiar to others. The history of
our State is a birthright which neither lands nor
gold can buy, for full as it is of stirring and pas-
sionate events, there is not an incident in our
annals that can bring the scarlet of shame to the
cheek of civilized man. Roger Williams, the first
settler, the thrice-exiled friend of the weak and
oppressed, by his revolt against Puritan intolerance
and his sacrifices for soul liberty, baptized Rhode
Island's early days with glory sufficient for any
State. It will be your pleasure to listen to-day to
one of his distinguished descendants in the person
of our orator. The red men, who warmly welcomed Williams to his haven of refuge, never af-
terwards had cause to accuse our people of torture, treachery or theft. Harassed and spurned as
Rhode Island was by the stronger colonies of New
England, she more than once stepped before the

angry hand of the Indian, when his blow could
have wiped from the land the early settlers of the
North.   Nor did any of the thirteen stars that first
formed the national constellation, shed with greater
brilliancy the light of freedom and liberty.   From
her sloops went the first shot at the wooden walls
of Britain and her sons were the foremost to shed
the blood which bought "a government of the
people, by the people and for the people."   Amid
those troublous hours, while struggling with pov-
erty within and foe without, she laid the founda-
tion of our American navy with one of her citizens as the commander-in-chief, and gave to the
Continental armies Nathanael Greene, an officer
second only to Washington.   The independent
spirit of her people which prompted her to be
the first to renounce allegiance to the mother
country, caused her to be cautious in entering the
uncertain restraints of the confederacy, but once
having thrown in her lot with the Union, no State
gave more freely of her life blood and treasure for
its preservation than "Little Rhody."   Among her
honored dead is the intrepid Commodore Perry,
who, after scattering the English squadron on Lake
Erie, wrote upon the records of American heroism
those inspiring words, "We have met the enemy
and they are ours."   Half a century later she sent

forth the gallant Burnside, and that brave band of blue, that rose from the farms and factory villages as promptly as the country called.

Many times since its settlement has the life of our little commonwealth been in jeopardy. Her faithful and friendly attitude towards the Indians, however, preserved not only her own existence but also that of neighboring colonies who were anxious to share her territory. The wine press of the revolution bruised her bitterly, and left her with commerce shattered and farms abandoned, but she welcomed to her midst Samuel Slater, who a little more than a century ago started the cotton industry which to-day is one of the principal sources of the State's wealth. Her contribution to the Civil War left her burdened with a heavy debt, which in a few months will be wiped out.

What Rhode Island is to-day, we invite you to see for yourselves. Our modest little building on these grounds speaks but of the size of her territory. Visit the machinery hall, and the noise of the engines and the whirl of the wheels from Rhode Island shall greet you at every turn. In the magnificent pavilion of manufactures you will see her famous workers in silver and you will find the choicest handiwork of her army of jewelers, and your attention will be attracted by the products of

our State's industry in woven goods of cotton, wool
and other fabrics.   Her women are well represented
in their departments and her hardy fishermen dis-
play the methods of their toil.   You are also invited to examine what she is doing for the younger
generation of her children in the direction of edu-
cating hand and mind.   She has taken of her best
and sent it hither in friendly rivalry with all the
world, and her exhibits not only reflect credit upon
her people but are a necessary complement of the
growing industries of this mighty nation.

It is my pleasurable duty, as governor, to welcome you all to join in our celebration.   You, who
have traversed the thousand miles which separate
us from home, need no utterance of mine to assure
you that you are welcome.   The laudable desire
to sustain the reputation of our State which has
prompted so many of you to come at this time
is greatly appreciated.

To you, sons and daughters of Rhode Island,
who have sought in these glorious western lands a
wider sphere for your ability and energy, I extend
that large hearted welcome with which you were
familiar in your early days.   We know the honor
of your native State has been carefully guarded in
your new-found homes and that your love for the
banner of "Hope" is no less than your loyalty to
the red, white and blue.

Right welcome, indeed, are you, our friends from other States, children with us of a common country. Rhode Island citizens claim it no small glory, that while preserving their individuality as a State, they may share with you the glorious heritage which our forefathers fought to secure. And no less hearty is our greeting to you, our friends of other lands, guests of this vigorous nation. We are honored by your presence to-day, and as we rejoice in the federation of States, so we look forward with hope to the federation of the world, which is typified in the grand spectacle spread before us.

But our acquaintance must not cease with to-day. Come to us when the summer sun is shining and the soft breezes are blowing from the ocean and we will unveil to you a landscape of bay and shore, of field and grove, whose beauties shall enrapture, and drive from your brow the clouds of care. We will fascinate you with the charms, the comforts and pleasures of our summer homes. We will also take you to the most populous hive of industry this nation knows; we will show you large and comfortable factories; we will show you prosperous homes of artisans "cunning to work in gold, and in silver, and in brass, and in iron, and in purple, and in crimson and blue and that can skill to grave." We will welcome you to a community animated with a

spirit of push and enterprise that will delight even
the active city under whose genial guardianship we
are gathered to-day.

Music:

MEXICAN BAND AND HUNGARIAN ORCHESTRA.

Oration.

PROFESSOR ALONZO WILLIAMS.

Your Excellency, Ladies and Gentlemen :—It marks
an epoch in the history of a State when it pauses a
day to conquer forgetfulness. A man who has arrived at full maturity, at a clear conception of his
relations, his duties, his mission, pauses to retrace
the arduous steps, the struggles, the defeats, the
triumphs, which have brought him to the threshold
of his desires, that he may pluck inspiration from
the past and gird himself for the future that invites
him. Thus pauses to-day our State and runs back
the checkered centuries to gather up the scattered
rays of her glory, that they may illumine the path
she is destined henceforth to tread.

Weak-winged are words, indeed, to climb the
height of such a theme, to do justice to such a day.
All attempt at learned historical discourse is beyond
the preparation of the speaker and undesired by you.
Any statistical array of the elements that make up
the record of our glory would scarcely be warranted

by the time your patience grants. The utmost I
may attempt, is to trace the main outlines of the
wondrous development of this Republic, and call
your attention to the distinguished part Rhode
Island has played in the high mission to which
this people has been called ; and I shall count my-
self happy if, under the inspiration of this presence
and of the dignity of this occasion, I may throw
such outlines upon the canvas as will enable you to
fill in the details and add the colors to the picture.

THE REPUBLIC. ITS MISSION.

We stand to-day upon the crest of the centuries.
The history and achievements of four hundred years
pass in majestic procession before the bewildered
gaze until we are lost in admiration and amazement and awe; the era of discoveries, crowded with
adventure and emblazoned with the names of those
hardy mariners of Spain and France and England,
whose brave keels cut on Vinland sands the first
runes in the great Saga of the West; the era of
colonization, pregnant with such mighty issues and
adorned with such mighty names, men of old,

> " Now ancient like the gods
> And safe as stars in all men's memories ;"

the era of the revolution, when only heroes lived ;

the critical era of confederation ; the long struggle
for national life under the Constitution and for the
Union, which so nearly ended in the greatest trag-
edy in history. These pages read to-day like the
books of a grand Homeric Epos. Every hour has
been an hour of splendid destiny. Every era has
been an era of splendid triumph. The entire record
is resplendent with brilliant achievements, which
hold captive the admiration of the world, and the
crowned result, upon which we gaze to-day, sur-
passes the incredulous tales of the romancers of old
and out runs the swiftest reach of apprehension.

DIVINE MISSION.

Who, that is conversant with this record, crowded
with the destinies of a world, can escape the con-
viction that this land was selected, this people
chosen, this Republic established for the accom-
plishment of a divine mission? "America is a last
effort of Divine Providence in behalf of the human
race," writes the sage of Concord. The history of
America is in itself a liberal education and should
henceforth occupy a leading place in the curricu-
lum of our common schools. The study of the
history of such a nation, its birth, its development,
its mission, imparts genuine culture, enlarges the
horizon of the soul, gives confidence in the perma-

nence and continuity of human institutions, faith
in an overruling Providence, and lifts us to that
high plane of contemplation where inspiration is
inhaled.

Political students aver that the causes which have
wrought in America such stupendous and unpar-
alleled results, are these: The topographical and
climatic conditions, the ethnic character of the people, and the moulding influence of its political institutions.

A land embracing climatic conditions so varied
that everything necessary for civilized man can be
readily produced; vast central plains sloping from
mountain chains on the east and the west, and
watered by streams that flow together into one
valley of three times a million square miles in
extent; eighty thousand miles of navigable river
banks, exceeding five fold those of Europe entire;
a chain of inland seas, carrying one-half nearly the
fresh water of the globe; a coast line of fourteen
thousand miles, affording harbors on two oceans
and unsurpassed—was ever race cradled in such a
land? The very face of its map, the contour of its
vast areas, the solid ribs of granite which bind them
together, its affluent and confluent streams, all pro-
claim, as by divine decree, the unity, the political
integrity of the Republic; and the rich elements

of soil and climate conspire to fulfill the destiny of the nation. "America is," indeed, "but another name for opportunity."

Moreover, the ethnic character of a people was never more suitably adapted to its physical environment and to its political mission than that of the dominant race in the New World. That grand struggle for supremacy in the beginning was the first crucial test in our history. Then and there was decided the fate of this Republic. The son of the Teuton prevailed over the descendant of the Roman. Arminius, not Cæsar, in Liberty's royal line, is the ancestor of Washington and Lincoln. Had the Saxon succumbed, this Republic could not have been, for from the forests of Ancient Germania we inherited the germs of free institutions. The pregnant import of that early struggle cannot be overestimated. No class of men probably *ever* made a greater change in the fortunes of mankind than those hardy, tenacious vikings of the sixteenth century. Their daring expeditions altered the destiny of the American continent, and thereby the career of the human race; and the record of their deeds has all the vigor and raciness of romance and the charm of poetry.

But the form of our political institutions is at once the chief cause of our prosperity and the proudest result of our endeavor. "A government of the people, by the people and for the people" is the one product which we exhibit with greatest pride in this Columbian year. This has been the mainspring and the chief cause of our marvellous development. Freedom liberates manhood, genius, inspiration, and from these flow material prosperity, social order, intellectual activity. The moulding influence of a government founded upon the equality of the individual has in this country wrought miracles such as ne'er before surprised the Muse of History. The stranger comes to us a serf and is made a freeman, he comes a subject and is invited to become a ruler, he comes ignorant and is made an intellectual peer, he comes poor and is made rich. Thus by the magic of freedom and opportunity a perilous heterogeneity is transmuted into a solid homogeneity, bound by the ties of a common interest and fused by the ardor of a common aspiration.

MATERIAL PROSPERITY.

In material prosperity, behold, whether we have been worthy of our splendid opportunity, worthy of our noble ancestry, worthy of the liberty we enjoy. Vast as is that subject, touch it at a few points where America leads the world; in agri-

culture, in manufactures, in mining, in the application of science to industry and art, in wealth.
Who dare quote statistics? The advance along
these lines is so tremendous that ere the echo of
our words has died away upon the air, the increase
has already been so marvellous that the speaker is
behind the times.

In agriculture America has in a century marched
from the rear to the head of the column, and even
Russia is second only *longo intervallo*. Nature has
lavished her bounties upon this land in a manner
that is absolutely prodigal, and we have not failed
to appreciate her favor. One quarter our total capital is invested in agriculture. I dare not state the
thousands of millions, lest you discredit me or the
figures daze the mind and paralyze the imagination.
One quarter of our total industrial product she
yields, and she claims the services of more than
two-fifths of all our laborers. We of the East do
not always appreciate the magnitude and the dignity of this, our most important industry. From
the beginning of civilization, Ceres has been the
goddess under whose benign influence has developed not material prosperity alone, but the rights
of property, then home, then government, then
culture and art; and all the divinities, from Ter-
minus and Themis to Apollo and the Graces, have

gladly followed the triumphal chariot of the triple turreted queen.

Not only in the soil, but beneath the soil, our supremacy is easy. Under waving fields of golden grain are endless chambers stored with treasures such as Aladdin's lamp ne'er disclosed, of gold, of silver, of copper, of iron, of coal, in quality and quantity elsewhere unknown.

In manufactures America leads the world, and employs three and one-half millions skilled workmen.

Again, in the application of science to industry and art America has no competitor. To say that steam and electricity were first harnessed to our chariot, to say that the majority of inventions growing out of their uses, the telegraph, the telephone, electric lighting, and a thousand others, are all offspring of the American brain, that one-half all the iron rails laid on the earth are laid in America, that one quarter all the telegraph wires are stretched above our heads, to say this, and similar things, means something, but when we think of all the hurrying traffic and ceaseless industries these represent, when we think of the millions of skilled and intelligent laborers to whom all this furnishes employment, high wages and happy homes, *then* our admiration for America and her industries begins.

It goes without saying, America leads the nations
in wealth. SIXTY THOUSAND MILLIONS! Comprehend it? Ah me! Herbert Spencer need not run
so far afield into the "Unknowable" to search out
that which passes the human understanding. We
collect these statistics, we write them down in figures, we repeat them in words, we print them in
books, but they convey no definite meaning even
to the tutored mind.

In the so called higher forms of intellectual activity, Europeans deny us still a rank, in literature,
in art, in refinement and culture. In place of these
we have, however, that which we could ill afford
to exchange for all their treasures. Much has been
done along these very lines of which we are justly
proud, but the hot, the impetuous intellectual life
of America has poured itself into other moulds, into
conquest of our domain, into manufactures, into railroads, into cities, into commonwealths. The glory
of action, the triumphs of life, not the seclusion of
letters, have been our inspiration and carried captive our best genius. Intellectual power? Yes! and
of the very best, original, creative power, has gone,
not into Iliads and Infernos, but into shorter roads
to commodious and noble living, into universal education, into states and constitutions. These, too,
have value and virtue, no less than epics and

dramas and Sistine Chapels, and to exchange the
Declaration of Independence for a Divina Comme-
dia, were the exchange of the golden armor of
Glaucus for the brazen armor of Diomede.

Ladies and gentlemen! Such are some of the
glories of America : a land teeming with hidden
treasures ; a land possessing one-half the railroads,
one-third the mining, one-quarter the manufactures, one-quarter the agriculture, one-quarter the
telegraph wires, one-sixth the wealth of the entire
globe ; a land occupied by sixty-five millions of the
best fed, best clothed, best housed, best paid, best
educated people on God's footstool ; a land with an
invested capital of untold millions, spending upon
education six times as much *per capita* as Europe,
with twelve million happy children in its public
schools, with four hundred colleges and universi-
ties for men, and two hundred for women (for it is
in America that woman is at last attaining to that
higher intellectual life which she so well adorns),
and five hundred schools of law, and medicine and
theology and science ; a land where the government
rests upon the liberty and equality of the governed ;
who is not proud to be a citizen, a king, in such a
Republic !

RHODE ISLAND. HER PART.

What part has Rhode Island played in this mighty drama? By what virtue is she entitled to a front seat in this great Congress of commonwealths? Were it not more modest in such a little State to sit unheard and let Massachusetts and New York and Virginia tell how THEY prepared the country and shaped its early destiny; and let the great west show the assembled nations how big we have come to be? Yes, were States measured by the league and heroic achievements weighed by silver and gold. This is Rhode Island Day, and yet we would not boast. The record unadorned is enough to show that our colony assumed from the first a unique position, and that in more than one important crisis in our history Rhode Island has proved herself something more than a peer of her sisters.

ROGER WILLIAMS.

At the risk of an anti-climax, let us mention our greatest glory first: the principle upon which our State was founded and the character of the founder, Roger Williams. Here Rhode Island stands alone, without a rival, and with just pride we may re-read to-day this title page in our history and recall the

glorious triumph of our great founder in his solitary
struggle in the cause of spiritual freedom. The
compact signed by the Pilgrims on the Mayflower
is bepraised as the first attempt to establish a government on the basis of the general good. Shall
the covenant subscribed by the first settlers of
Providence occupy in history a less honorable
place? In the valley of the Mooshausic, on the
hills where you dwell, for *the first time in history* was
set up a government on the basis of religious liberty. *There* came into being a political community
which was an anomaly among the nations, a pure
democracy, but "*only in civil things*," so reads the
covenant. And this thing was done in little Rhode
Island. Nay more, this Rhode Island idea, as it
was derisively called, has become the accepted and
fundamental maxim of American politics, and has
been incorporated into the constitution of every
State. Even Massachusetts has deigned to tread
the path cleared in the wilderness by her great
exile, though strange as it seems, she waited two
centuries ere working out a complete divorce of
Church and State, and up to 1833 her citizens were
taxed for the support of the church. No one principle of political or social or religious polity lies
nearer the base of American institutions and has
done more to shape our career than this principle

inherited from Rhode Island, and it may be asserted
that the future of America was in a large measure
determined by that General Court which summoned
Roger Williams to answer for "divers *new* and *dan-
gerous* opinions," and his banishment became "a
pivotal act in universal history." Are we boasting,
or are we just reading the record, and that too,
without much emphasis?

Personally Roger Williams was no ordinary man.
While his never-failing sweetness of temper and
unquestioned piety won for him the warmest affection even of his opponents, yet he was a man of
stern parts,

> "Limbed like the old heroic breeds,
>   Who stand self-poised on manhood's earth,
>   Not forced to frame excuses for his birth,
>   Fed from within with all the strength he needs;"

he was a man of unyielding tenacity of purpose, a
man who grasped clearly a principle in all its bearing and could incorporate it in a social compact.
Moreover, he was no crude, unlearned agitator, but
a scholar and thinker. On the roll of the ancient
Charter House in London will be found his name
among the first, above those of Addison and Steele,
of Wesley and Blackstone, of Grote and Thack-
eray. He was a graduate of Cambridge, an eloquent preacher, an intimate friend of Sir Harry

Vane, a teacher of Milton. Behold it! the author of Paradise Lost sitting at the feet of the author of Soul-Liberty. Not only his learning, but his versatility was extraordinary. He was by turns, reporter, preacher, trader, farmer, scholar, diplomat, linguist, teacher, legislator, judge, soldier, man of letters. He was a stalwart, even among the intellectual giants of those early days, when men thought great thoughts. He stands alone in American history, the only one of his kind, and he belongs to Rhode Island. Such is her unique glory, Roger Williams and Religious Liberty, and this alone were enough to immortalize one State.

THE ERA OF THE REVOLUTION.

Glance at another era, the period of the Revolution. Did you ever count upon the fingers the matters of grave importance in which Rhode Island was first, *facile princeps?*

She was the first to instruct her officers to disregard the Stamp Act and to ensure them indemnity for so doing.[1]

She was first to support the resolutions passed by the House of Burgesses in Virginia in 1769, declaring that in them alone was vested the right

---

[1] Arnold, Hist. R. I., II., 261, 286.

of taxation.   Rhode Island had explicitly declared the same thing four years earlier.[1]

The people of Providence in town meeting assembled was the first authorized body to recommend the permanent establishment of a Continental Congress,[2] and the General Assembly of Rhode Island was the first to appoint delegates thereto.[3]

Rhode Island formally enacted and declared her independence of Great Britain two months before the Declaration of Independence by Congress.   She is thus the oldest independent sovereign government in the western world.[4]

Rhode Island was first to brave royalty in arms, and she spilled the first blood in the war for independence.   Before Lexington,[5] even before the famous Boston "Tea Party,"[6] men of Newport had sunk His Royal Majesty's armed sloop Liberty,[7] and men of Providence had sent up the Gaspee in flames.[8]

Rhode Island was the first to establish a naval armament in America, she fired the first cannon

---

[1] Arnold, Hist. R. I., II., 295, 286.

[2] May 17, 1774. Arnold, Hist. R. I., II., 334.

[3] Samuel Ward and Esek Hopkins, June 15, 1774. Arnold, Hist. R. I., II., 336.

[4] May 4, 1776. Arnold, Hist. R. I., II., 273. R. I. Col. Rec. VII., 522.

[5] Lexington, April 19, 1775.   [6] Boston "Tea Party," Dec. 16, 1773.

[7] July 19, 1769. Arnold, Hist. R. I., II., 297.

[8] June 9-10, 1772. Arnold, Hist. R. I., II., 312, 317-318.

at the royal navy, she captured the first prize,[1] she was the first to recommend and urge upon Congress the establishment of a Continental Navy, she was chosen to execute the plans,[2] our townsman, Esek Hopkins, was the first Commander-in-Chief, (then so called) and three fourths of all the officers were from the little State of Rhode Island, whose bold mariners were the very vikings of the American Revolution.[3]

Again, in proportion to her size and population, none of the thirteen States can compare with little Rhode Island in contributions to the Continental Loan. I cannot resist the persuasion to pause just a moment to emphasize that important item. We all know how vital to success are the sinews of war, not only of loyal men, but none the less of *money*. Bitter experience has taught us this, in our own day and generation. Who was it during that long and critical struggle, who unlocked their private treasures and poured them like water into the common cause for independence, and that, too, without hope of return? The loyal patriotic citizens of Rhode Island! Though her State treasury was exhausted and largely in debt, by reason of expenses incurred during the French war, yet how

---

[1] June 15, 1775. Arnold, Hist. R. I., II., 350-351.

[2] Arnold, Hist. R. I., II., 355-356. [3] Arnold, Hist. R. I., II., 362.

nobly, how generously, how patriotically, she responded to the urgent call, history bears witness. The accounts of the Continental Loan Office, in 1783, show that only four States had contributed more than Rhode Island, diminutive though she was. Read the glorious account: Maryland, four times as populous, Rhode Island contributes one and a half times as much; a ratio of six to one. Virginia, eight times as populous, Rhode Island contributes twice as much; a ratio of sixteen to one. North Carolina, three times as populous, Rhode Island contributes six times as much; a ratio of eighteen to one. South Carolina, three times as populous, Rhode Island contributes seven times as much; a ratio of twenty-one to one. Because Rhode Island hesitated to surrender to the Federal government the liberties enjoyed under her charter, the most liberal ever granted to a colony, shall detractors still continue to charge her with a lack of patriotism? History answers. The balance sheet of that Continental Loan Account, made up by the Board of Commissioners appointed by Congress in 1789, hung up before you on the walls of this auditorium, were in itself alone eloquent enough for an address on this historic occasion.[1]

---

[1] Madison Papers, Gilpin's Ed., 364, 431. Baucroft's Hist. Const. U. S., 81. Pitkin's Pol. and Civ. Hist. U. S., 346, 538.

Again, Rhode Island contributed not only as much money, but also proportionally as many men, to the common cause, as any State, and they fought in every great battle under Washington during the war,' while Springfield and Red Bank and Quaker Hill, and especially Trenton Bridge, showed the stuff of which they were made. Nor must we forget to add that in the field Nathanael Greene was second only to Washington, and in the councils of the nation Stephen Hopkins was second to none.

I forbear, lest there be nothing of the first grade during this period left for the other States. Massachusetts has been especially fortunate in the unusually large number of brilliant men of letters who have devoted their lives to the happy task of singing her praise and of embalming in prose and verse the immortal achievements with which her career is crowded. "O fortunate youth," said Alexander, as he stood by the tomb of Achilles in Sigeum, "O fortunate youth, who found Homer as the herald of thy virtues. For had there been no Iliad, the same tomb which covered thy body would have buried also thy name." Rhode Island has not been wanting in first things and great deeds, but Massachusetts has been more than rich in the heralds of her virtue.

' Staples' R. I. in Cont. Cong., 400.

THE PRESENT CENTURY.

This hour would hardly permit us to point out how nobly Rhode Island has borne herself in times of peace and in times of war during the present century. "We have met the enemy and they are ours" was the watchword from Rhode Island in 1812. Twenty-four thousand loyal sons, led by that ideal soldier, the hero *sans peur et sans reproche*, Ambrose E. Burnside, was Rhode Island's contribution to the nation in 1861. In the arts of peace, our State has from the very beginning occupied a prominent position : in cotton, in woolen and worsteds, in jewelry, in thread, in machinery, in engines, in screws, in silver; and in more than one of these industries she leads the world. Even Attleboro and Newark as centres for the manufacture of jewelry can hardly be mentioned beside Providence, with its 167 separate establishments, and ten millions of capital; and Birmingham, Moscow and Odessa are but small affairs in comparison. Moreover, no establishment for the manufacture of silver in the world can be mentioned at the same moment with Gorham's. In the manufacture of cotton Rhode Island may lay claim to a peculiar honor, for it was she who laid the foundations of this great American industry. Samuel Slater, the

"Father of American Manufactures," as President
Jackson named him, set up his Arkwright machinery in Pawtucket in the year 1790, and by
forty-five years of unremitting toil built up an
industry unequalled in his day, planting mills all
over Rhode Island, Massachusetts, Connecticut and
New Hampshire, and from him went out skilled
workmen to establish the manufacture of cotton
all over this land. Over one-half of the capital of
the State is to-day invested in this industry, and
one corporation, the largest in the world, renders
its dozen villages musical with the hum of 421,000
spindles, and makes them beautiful by the happi-
ness of more than 7,000 operatives.

FAITH.

Ladies and gentlemen ! The year eighteen hundred and ninety-three witnesses in our land a re-
birth of patriotism, a renaissance of nationality.
This is our golden jubilee, and we invite our kin
of all the earth to celebrate with us our festival
and behold how the God of the nations has blessed
this people.

On this four hundredth anniversary we raise
our national hero in marble, in silver, in gold, to
the pedestal in the national pantheon beside the
immortals of the Columbian race : *Columbus*, the

discoverer; *Washington*, the father; *Lincoln*, the
savior of his country!

These, our national heroes, typify that element of
character which has inspired the American people
through the struggle of the centuries to this tri-
umphant issue, *Faith:* the highest, the deepest, the
most potent power that moves man or nations to
supremest action; *Faith*, that element of moral
character which dominated all others in each of
these heroes; faith in a divine ruler, faith in a
divine mission, faith in themselves; a faith that
enabled them to stand self-poised among men, a
faith unwavering in their convictions of truth and
duty; a faith that discerned a light in the dark-
ness, when other men saw only into night and
gloom; a faith that credentialed their divine mission among men.

What we honor most in the man Columbus is
his sublime *faith*; a faith that all the superstition
and credulity of the 15th century could not under-
mine; a faith that all the ignorance of learning
and science could not shake; a faith that all the
indifference and insults and treachery of kings
and courts could not discourage; a faith so fine, so
spiritual that it was counted madness and delusion;
a faith so keen that it imparted the divination of
genius and prophecy; a faith so strong, so insistent

that had there been no New World, God would have created one for him to discover.

This faith is the key-note of American history. Faith it was, that led the early colonists to plant the seeds of a new civilization upon the hard, forbidding coast of New England. Faith it was, that led Roger Williams into the wilderness, that he might establish for mankind the principle of spiritual-liberty. Faith it was, that led our fathers through struggle to liberty and independence. Faith it was, that in our day led this people, under our great martyr-hero, through the Red Sea of civil strife into the land of promise which we to-day enjoy. Faith it is, that to-day moves the wheels of all our industries and enables us to invite the nations of the earth to gaze upon a spectacle in this queen city of the West such as the sun in his eternal course never before shone upon. It is faith, a faith that is optimistic, faith in God, faith in man, faith in the sublime mission of this country. *Faith* has ever been and is to-day the central fact in American civilization, running like a golden thread through all the warp and woof of that grand tapestry we have been weaving on the great loom of the centuries, emblazoned with the birth and triumphs of a nation, and pictured with the lives of its heroes and saints and martyrs.

Let us learn this lesson from the past: *Faith!* When pessimism encroaches upon optimism, when anarchy defies law, when political or financial or social dangers gather about us, when pilots are faithless, and timid or treacherous men are at the helm ; *then*, inspired by the matchless achievements of a glorious past, aroused to noblest effort by the opportunities of a splendid present; *then*, like our hero, Columbus, with an unwavering faith in our hearts, a faith in the divine mission to which this nation has been called, a faith that the land of freedom and prosperity is before us, let us plant ourselves upright and firm upon the prow of the ship, and keep our eye fixed firmly upon the bright star of hope in the West that still beckons us, on, on !

Music: Newport Band.

8

Poem.

READ BY COL. JOHN C. WYMAN.

RHODE ISLAND'S GIFT

Last of the thirteen, smallest of them all,
What canst thou bring to this World's Festival,
Where all thy sisters come with pride and power,
And bring each one a Princess' generous dower
Of gold and gems, and fruits, and precious woods,
And joyous tribute of their costly goods.

  The wild Atlantic beats thy shore,
    The fleecy sea fog folds thee round,
  Point Judith counts its wrecks by score,
    Where stately ships their graves have found.
  The Seekonk takes its shining way
    Past swelling hills of tender green,
  To where the waters of the bay
    Bask softly in their silver sheen.

So small a State that it is true
   From any top of highest hill,
Another State still comes to view
   To give the gazing eye its fill.

What can we bring?   No outward show of gain,
No pomp of state ; we bring the sons of men !
The man who lived two centuries ago
In persecutions which set hearts aglow,
Who dared to say when every where, world wide,
Men made belief and state-craft coincide,
" We have no law to punish or disperse
Those who express their faith in ways diverse ;"
Successors to that man, full well may dare
To claim they are a prophet's lawful heir.
These many years to us there have not failed
Some lofty spirits with whom truth prevailed,
Who stood for right, the high, the ideal things,
Until this freedom with its healing wings
Spread over all the land, and now the whole
From East to West has the Rhode Island soul.

   Bring gold, fair sisters, yellow gold,
      And gems and all that's fair and fine,
   And heap them all, the new, the old,
      Before our country's stately shrine.
   Bring hardihood from north and east,

Bring beauty from the south and west,
Bring valor to adorn the feast,
Bring all that has withstood time's test.
We grudge you not the riches rare,
We grudge you not your acres broad ;
We bring you for our noble share
THE LIBERTY TO WORSHIP GOD.

—Caroline Hazard.

Music: Mexican Band.

Address.

THE SONS OF RHODE ISLAND

Col. William A. James.

We stand to-day in the presence of the largest representation of the people of the earth and of its resources, the products of human industries and the inventions that have been gathered together.

It is wonderful in magnitude and excellence, and the coöperation of the whole world was needed to produce it. Much labor and study are required to comprehend it, and it will pass into history as the Exposition beyond which no city, state or nation will ever attempt to go. It has been one of the features of the Fair to arrange for special days to be called "State Days," and to-day is Rhode Island's day, and hundreds of her citizens have assembled to make it a success.

The great states of New York, Pennsylvania, Illi-

nois, Ohio and Indiana, with Iowa and Massachusetts, have had their days. All great and wonderful
states, of which we are proud. Our great state of
Illinois is an empire. Situated in the valley of
the Mississippi, whose waters flow along its westerly
borders for nearly seven degrees of latitude, it com-
prises an area of territory more than that of the
whole New England states. While all this is true,
it is also true that, while Rhode Island does not
cut a very big figure on the map of the American
Republic, the traveler who leaves Rhode Island
out of his route can tell you but little of what the
American people are.

It was once said by a distinguished Rhode Islander in Congress, in response to some derogatory
remarks regarding the dimensions of our little
state, that "what the eye is to the elephant, Rhode
Island is to the Union." I think it was Doesticks
who says that he visited the state of Connecticut
and that he had walked around the state of Rhode
Island before breakfast. In speaking of his experience he said that "if Connecticut is the land of
'wooden nutmegs,' Rhode Island is the greater
(grater)." We are all proud of Rhode Island, of
her splendid material development, of her wonderful resources and all that goes to make a state rich
and great and her people happy. We are prouder

still of the achievements of her sons and daughters. The impress of the genius of her sons is upon the pages of our country's history.

In the long line of distinguished Rhode Islanders, let me speak of General Nathanael Greene, that patriot of Revolutionary fame, second only to General Washington as a general and a hero, whose name will live as long as the American Revolution is remembered.

General Ambrose E. Burnside, whom every Rhode Islander loved, whose memory is still dear to us all, who won the praise of every lover of his country for his military achievements. Let me speak of General Rodman, Colonel Slocum, Major Sullivan Ballou, of Ives, Turner, Shaw and Curtis, and the numberless Rhode Island heroes who gave their lives in support of the Union. At the head of this great Exposition stands a man of iron nerve, of great executive ability (as you know he must be), of wonderful resources, known as the Director General, George R. Davis. We claim him as a Rhode Islander, as he was an officer in a Rhode Island regiment during the war of '61-65. Now as to the Sons and Daughters of Rhode Island in Chicago, I wish to say we have an organization and a membership of about one hundred.

We have in our membership the son of an ex-

governor of Rhode Island, a former president of
the common council of Providence, the son of a
former speaker of the House of Representatives of
Rhode Island.   In our membership you will find
the names of Francis, Ballou, Chace, Angell, Tay-
lor, Belden, Cozzens, Waterman, Cragin, Wolcott,
Peckham, and others, all good Rhode Island names
with which you are familiar.   I can say that the
Rhode Islanders living in Chicago have done their
part to make this great city by the murmuring
waters of Lake Michigan what it is, the wonder
and admiration of the world.   In behalf of the
Sons and Daughters of Rhode Island, I can say
we are glad to see you, and give you a right royal
welcome.   May your stay be pleasant and profitable.

Music : Newport Band.

Poem.

By Henry Robinson Palmer.

Though by Michigan we stray,
　Yet our constant thought to-day
Stealeth swift across the mountains
　Back to Narragansett Bay ;
　To its hill-tops flushing fair,
　In the sweet Atlantic air,
And the dear and gracious Mother
　In her beauty seated there.

If our footsteps we retrace
　To the old abiding place,
What a joy of welcome shineth
　In her calm and kindly face !
　When they catch the smile that slips
　For a greeting from her lips,
Then her sons and daughters love her
　To her dainty finger tips.

9

Though but scanty be her fields,
Yet a broader sway she wields,
Reaching out from sea to prairie,
In the children that she yields.
Aye, a very queen is she,
As the dullest eye may see,
And her loftiest dominion
In our loyal hearts shall be.

Nor, forsooth, shall we confess,
That we cherish her the less,
If we turn us to her sisters
And the plenty they possess.
Nay, our love shall not abate,
For our hearts are consecrate
To the faith that gave her freedom
And the hope that made her great.

Here we hail the happy age
Blazoned on Rhode Island's page;
Like a beacon-flame to guide us
Be that ancient heritage!
Though the years course o'er us fast,
Yet the sweet and sturdy past
In our memories shall linger,
Like an echo to the last.

*　　*　　*　　*　　*

This fair city, wondrous made,
　As by miracle uplaid,
With its lofty domes and towers,
　As by miracle will fade.
　And its waves will no more gleam,
　And its shining walls will seem
Like the bright and hallowed glory
　Of a well-remembered dream ;

But though all its beauties wane,
　And our fond regrets be vain,
Still the faith and hope that built it
　In the common State remain.
　Let her walls like these arise,
　Pure and white to greet the skies,
And the sight shall stir the spirit,
　And be sweet unto the eyes.

Music: Mexican Band.

Address.

COL. JOHN C. WYMAN.

You are all aware that we Rhode Islanders, while we recognize that ours is the smallest State in the Union, being cognizant of how important a factor she has always been in our country's history, can but feel an honorable pride in recalling and reviewing her past record, and that we claim for her a prominent position in this marvel of the nineteenth century, the World's Columbian Exposition.

You know we have a game bird which has a national and, I may say, an international reputation. The Rhode Island turkey is known and approved everywhere, but while superior to all other turkeys in flavor, it is about the same in formation, and is not all breast. You have already had Rhode Island served you till all the best, I fear, has been distributed, and you must bear with and excuse me if, in the preparation of the dish I have to furnish, you now and then discover a familiar chestnut.

I have attended several of these ceremonial occasions known as State Days, and have observed that it is almost invariably claimed by the State commemorating, that she was the first in the Union, that she had larger resources (undeveloped in some instances), was of more importance to the Union than any other, and that but for her possibly there might never have been a Union, certainly never one comparing with the one we have in extent, intelligence and influence. Now all this is as true of Rhode Island as it is of the other States who have claimed it, and it is not necessary for me, familiar as you are with her past history, to spend any time in establishing her right to be regarded as worthy to rank with any of the thirteen original States, who declared, defended and demonstrated their right to an independent form of government.

But in the presence of this magnificent exhibition, where Genius has taken its highest flight and man has shown himself capable of greater and grander achievements than have ever been accomplished before, since the first morning in Eden, Rhode Islanders may well be proud to say, "It was the founder of their State who first asserted and established the right of absolute religious liberty," and here let me state a very interesting fact.

The Convention first called by the three Rhode Island Colonies to take steps to secure a Charter

met at Aquidnick. It was then agreed to apply to
England for a Charter and Roger Williams was
duly elected to secure the same, on September 19th,
1643.

The call for the World's Parliament of Religions
was issued and the Committee organized September
19th, 1893, just two hundred and fifty years later.
Now mark this : On the arch over the right column
of the Peristyle are these words, studiously selected,
" Toleration in Religion the best fruit of the last
four Centuries."

We are to-day precisely where Roger Williams
was two hundred and fifty years ago when he ad-
vocated and illustrated this same sentiment. What
grander claim could we make to royal recognition
than to have furnished such a man?"

While it may be that none of us may enter
the Promised Land, which will unquestionably be
reached when all Sectarianism is abolished, and
people come together on the broad platform of love
for man and worship for God,—what changes will
come to the world then,—and while we may not see
those changes, while we may not ourselves be ben-
efited by them, our duty is none the less obligatory
to strive for that religious tolerance which will
produce them. Moses sought and struggled during
forty years, strengthened and sustained by the hope

of entering the Land of Promise, and after all he was permitted only to stand upon the top of Pisgah and look upon what he could neither enter nor enjoy. We must be content to stand on a moral Pisgah and as we catch glimpses of a better time which is sure to come, "learn to labor and to wait."

I believe that this is the dawn of a New Era, and if there shall be two, or one hundred years hence another World's Fair Exhibition, these great weapons of war, destruction, and death, which in this one excite so much interest and admiration, will be looked upon not only with wonder and amazement, but with as much horror and hatred as we now look upon the instruments of torture employed by the Inquisition. It seems to me this great Exposition is hastening the day when we shall no longer have occasion for death-dealing weapons. All the nations have been represented here, a better knowledge of each other has resulted, and if differences and difficulties arise between them, arbitrators and not "grim visaged war" will amicably arrange and settle them.

Much has been said of the rapid and wonderful material development of this Western World during the past two hundred years, but the time is coming and now is when a wiser appreciation of what tends to highest development of the race will obtain and men will begin to understand the spiritual significance of this great exhibit of the world's life; then people will begin to realize that there is something to do besides increase armies and navies or accumulate vast hoards of wealth to be squandered in selfish indulgence. We wonder at and admire Columbus as he sailed over a great and unknown ocean. We stand to-day as Columbus stood upon the deck of his ship, but we are gazing over a greater and more unknown ocean, the ocean of the world's moral future.

The great question of labor and capital; how to harmonize relations now so discordant and antagonistic; the question how best to equalize the conditions of the people of this earth; the question whether the palace and the slum must ever be near neighbors; these are the great issues that lie before us, and he who helps us to solve them is the true benefactor of his race even though he adds nothing to the material wealth of the country. I believe through this Exposition we are coming to a feeling of brotherhood such as we have never known before, and that we are going to get a better and clearer idea of religion than we have ever yet had. I believe we are going to find out with the great founder of our religion, that love for God must begin with love for man, and that there is no love for God until love for man has been developed, and when human hearts have learned this lesson, then

> " Waft, waft, ye winds, the story,
>   And you, ye waters, roll,
>   Till like a sea of glory
>   It spreads from pole to pole."

I feel sure that the dawn of this day has begun, and we are already marching toward that glorious period of universal peace and brotherhood.

> "Then let us pray that come it may,
>   As come it will for a' that,
>   When sense and worth o'er a' the earth,
>   Shall bear the gree, and a' that.
>   For a' that, and a' that,
>   It's coming yet, for a' that—
>   When man to man, the warld o'er,
>   Shall brothers be for a' that."

Music: Hungarian Orchestra.

Address.

HON. THOMAS W. PALMER.

President Palmer was not down upon the programme for an address, as his presence was a wholly unlooked for honor. Although his address was entirely impromptu, yet it was eloquent and deeply interesting. None of the daily papers gave an abstract of it, and it is now almost impossible to reproduce even a faint outline of it, and any attempt to re-present the brilliant flights of eloquence, or restore the delicate conceits in which the address abounded, would be wholly futile. Among other things President Palmer said: On no former occasion has the National Commission attended a State celebration in a body, but has reserved this special honor for Rhode Island, because, first, of its admiration and respect for Governor Brown, who has borne himself with such dignity, and won from all such high esteem since his arrival a week ago; and I personally, and the Commission as a body, desired to seize this opportunity to express by this official recognition our high regard for your State, for your Governor, and for the distinguished party of ladies and gentlemen who honor the Fair by their presence this day.

In order to emphasize this honor, which we desire to confer, we have marched hither in a body, and brought with us two bands of music, the Hungarian Orchestra and Mexican National Band, which has been sent to Chicago by President Diaz to participate in the exercises of Mexico Day, which occurred yesterday. This excellent musical organization of forty pieces we desire to place at the disposal of your Governor for the rest of the day and evening.

We all honor Rhode Island, not only because of her manufactures, her cotton mills, her skill in fashioning silver and gold, and her clams, but also because of her history, replete with great deeds and great men. I am proud of her especially because of my own generous lineage. I am what might properly be called a genealogical mosaic : a lineal descendant of Roger Williams, born in New Hampshire, educated in Ohio, and settled in Michigan. I am proud of Rhode Island also because the man who has done so much to make this great Columbian Exposition a success, a man of such wonderful executive ability, the Director General, George R. Davis, is a son of Rhode Island, and rendered heroic service during the Civil War as an officer from that

State. I am proud of Rhode Island, moreover, because of her heroes. of the past, of Roger Williams, of General Nathanael Greene, of Perry, of Burnside.

In conclusion, may I express the hope that the noble lessons taught by this Exposition may not perish, and that this great people will rise up and demand the preservation, at least, of the Court of Honor, that it may make this city the central city of the continent, to which all lovers of humanity can make pilgrimages and lay their offerings before the shrine of art.

At the close of President Palmer's eloquent address, the Newport Artillery rose in a body and gave three cheers for President Palmer and the National Commission. Not to be outdone, the Brown University Alumni present gave three Brown cheers, followed by a rah! rah! rah!

IV. DRESS PARADE

After the exercises in Music Hall, Col. Alvin A.
Barker tendered a complimentary Dress Parade to
His Excellency, Governor D. Russell Brown, on
the Administration Plaza. The Newport Artillery
paraded as a battalion of three companies, com-
manded respectively by Major George C. Shaw,
Lieut. John D. Richardson and Capt. Herbert
Bliss. The Newport Band, under the command
of Thomas W. Henry, furnished the music and attracted much attention by their beautiful white
uniform, while the military marches rendered
elicited much applause. The Drum Major, Mr.
Louis Shanteler, gained favorable comment by the
skilful manner in which he conducted the evolu-
tions of the band.

His Excellency was accompanied by his General
and Personal Staff and all the members of the
official party, and the Parade attracted immense
crowds from every direction, so that scarcely space
could be found in which to go through the marches

and counter-marches. The battalion, under the skilful handling of Colonel Barker and Adjutant Stevens, acquitted itself, however, in a most creditable manner. The movements of the companies and the exercises in the manual of arms were performed with a promptness and precision that called forth general admiration. His Excellency, Governor Brown, was especially pleased and took occasion to compliment the officers and men in words of highest praise. After the parade the Artillery Company marched to the Rhode Island Building, stacked arms, posted guard and waited for the services demanded of them in the evening.

V. EVENING RECEPTION

In the evening from seven to ten a reception was given by the Rhode Island Board of World's Fair Managers to His Excellency, D. Russell Brown, Governor of Rhode Island. Governor and Mrs. Brown were assisted in receiving by the ladies connected with the Commission. Guards from the Newport Artillery were stationed in and about the building, while the building and the lawn were elaborately decorated, and in most exquisite taste. The chief of the Fair decorations said that the building, with its many vari-colored lights, Japanese lanterns, flags, bunting, palms, exotics, garlands of flowers of all hues, and wreaths of rich foliage, could not be rivalled by any reception thus far given. A large pavilion had been pitched upon the rear lawn, in which refreshments were served. Many thousand ladies and gentlemen from Rhode Island were present during the evening, and a large number of distinguished officials of Chicago, and others connected with the Fair, called to pay their respects to Governor and Mrs. Brown.

Among others were the Executive Commissioners from Maine, Connecticut, New Hampshire, Massachusetts, New York, Virginia, Pennsylvania, Missouri, South Dakota, Washington, Indiana, Michigan, Illinois, and Ohio. The toilets of the ladies were very attractive and many of them superb, that of Mrs. Gov. Brown attracting special attention by its richness and beauty. The theme of the evening was the grand success of the day, and specially the exercises in Music Hall. The genial John C. Wyman, Executive Commissioner, was highly complimented by all for his tact and administrative skill and never-failing good nature, while the smoothness in the execution of the day's programme was credited by unanimous consent to the careful preparation and foresight of the Committee on Ceremonies under Chairman John P. Sanborn. The Newport Band was stationed upon the lawn in front of the building and during the evening gave a concert made up of classical pieces and patriotic airs which added much to the pleasure of the occasion. It was nearly midnight when the gay festivities were brought to a close.

Thus ended a day pronounced by all present a magnificent success from beginning to close, and by the Chicago press declared to be the most successful celebration held thus far on any State Day.

www.ingramcontent.com/pod-product-compliance
Lightning Source LLC
Chambersburg PA
CBHW021425090426
42742CB00009B/1253